The **Sophia Day**™ Creative Team-
Megan Johnson, Stephanie Strouse,
Kayla Pearson, Timothy Zowada, Mel Sauder

Published and Distributed by MVP Kids Media, LLC
Mesa, Arizona, USA
Printed by RR Donnelley Asia Printing Solutions, Ltd
Dongguan City, Guangdong Province, China
DOM Apr 2018, Job # 02-002-01

help me UNDERSTAND™

Feeling *Worry* & Learning *Comfort*™

REAL mvpkids®

Miriam Lassoes the Worry Whirlwind™

SOPHIA DAY™

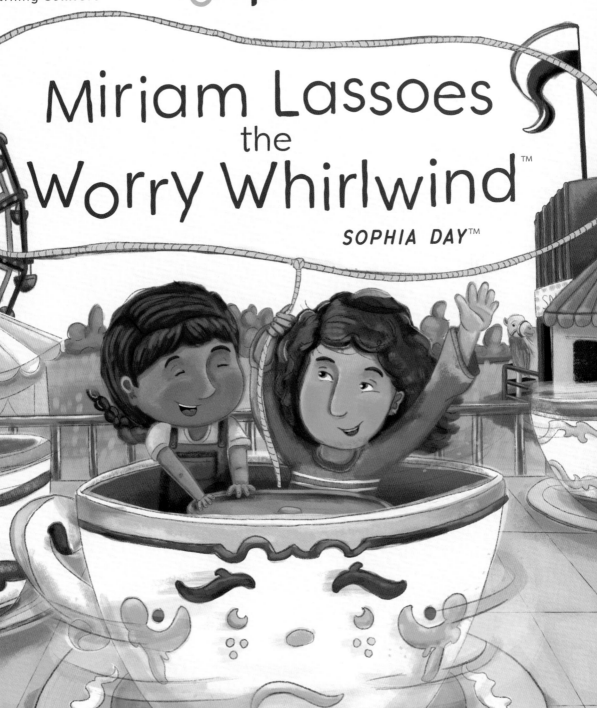

Written by Megan Johnson   Illustrated by Stephanie Strouse

Miriam and her family were on their way to the Royce County Fair. As they left the city skyline behind, **Miriam's excitement** shone like the sun!

Last year she wasn't tall enough to ride most of the rides, but this time she could ride them all!

But Miriam often worried.
She began to feel that worry whirlwind
rise up, swirling around in her mind like a storm.

What if the rides were *scarier* than she expected?
What if they *don't have* any food she likes?
What if she *loses* her shoes on the roller coaster?

"*Baba*," she called to her dad.
"Can people fall off of a Ferris wheel?
They're **SO** high up!"

* 'Amira' is an Arabic nickname meaning "princess."

"The rides are safe. You **won't** fall," he assured her.

"I think you'll like it a lot. Don't worry, *amira**."

But Miriam **was** worried.

He said "*won't*", but he didn't say "*can't*." Miriam was always thinking about words like that. Speaking more than one language makes a person notice words.

The worry whirlwind grew bigger.

She wondered if seat belts ever break.

What if she gets hit by a flying shoe?

Could animals get loose from their pen?

Could she get sick from eating too much cotton candy?

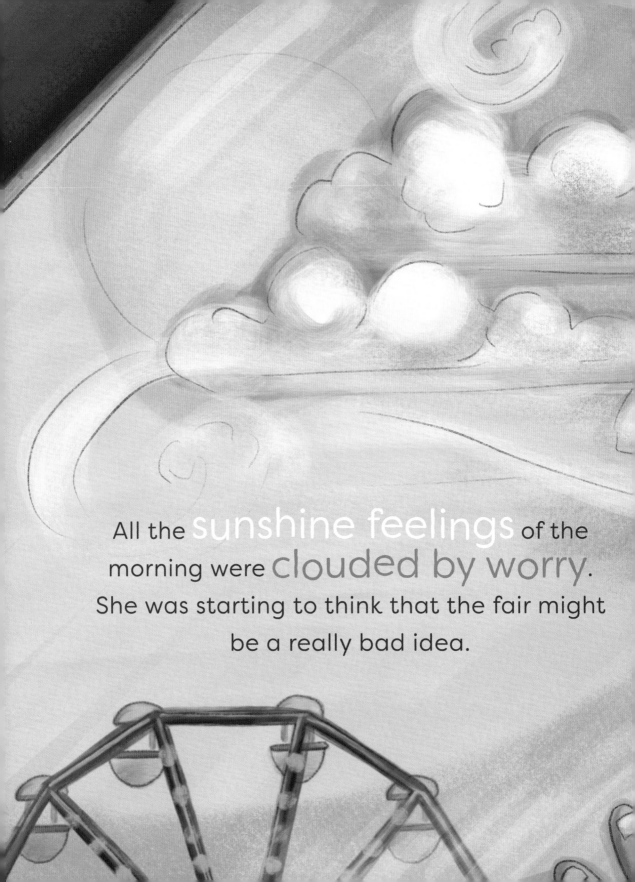

All the sunshine feelings of the morning were clouded by worry. She was starting to think that the fair might be a really bad idea.

As they got out of the car, the worry whirlwind moved from Miriam's' head to her belly, making her feel sick.

"Mama, I don't feel well," Miriam said. "Maybe we shouldn't stay long. Sara and Adam might get tired or hot, and we don't want them to get sick."

"Oh, Miriam, you sound worried. **Please trust us.** This will be a fun day if you keep your worry under control. We will keep you safe," her mom reassured her.

ROYCE COUNTY FAIR

TICKETS

"We'll work together, or else that little
worry whirlwind will become a
full-blown *sandstorm*!" her dad joked.

Miriam gave a nervous laugh.

She *imagined*
a GIANT sandstorm
swallowing up the whole County Fair.
Miriam experienced a sandstorm once
while visiting her cousins in the Arabian
Desert. The sand can be so thick you can't
see what's right in front of you!

Sometimes worries get that thick, too,
like a million grains of sand flying at a
hundred kilometers* per hour.

*A kilometer is a bit more than half a mile. Kilometers are used to
measure distance in most countries outside of the United States.

Miriam came back to reality. She wanted to see the petting zoo first since she didn't see many animals in the city.

"This place is so big. What if I get lost?" she asked her mom.

"Let's **LASSO** your worry.

LOOK AT THE FACTS. We've been coming here for years, and we've always stuck together. We have a responsibility to each other to stay close and we'll all do our part."

"If we do get separated, do you remember our safety plan?"

"Yes, Mama," Miriam replied. "Stay put and tell an adult with a badge."

"That's right," Mama replied. "The staff are trained to help anyone who is lost. You can take comfort in that. See, **all the facts line up**."

Miriam felt more confident as she took her mom's hand.

The petting zoo was in the far corner of the fairgrounds. They walked past so many rides along the way.

"You're tall enough for all these rides this year! Do you want to do this one on our way to the petting zoo?" Her mom gestured toward the spinning Whirly Cups.

Her stomach flipped as she watched the cups spin. It looked like fun, but *her mind swirled* with all the things that could go wrong.

She stood frozen,
unable to answer.

"Miriam, do you want to
try it? The line is short.
We could do this first."

Snapping out of her daydreams,
she answered dramatically, "I'll get sick!
I'll slip out and fly through the air!"
She could feel tears sting her eyes.

"We won't force you to ride anything, but you were so excited about it before.
Let's **LASSO** your **worry**, Miriam.
ASK THE RIGHT QUESTIONS," said Baba.

Miriam knew what he meant. Whenever Miriam felt anxious, her parents helped her **ask questions** to decide whether she should really be worried.

"What is the chance you would slip out of the seat belt if you follow the rules?" Mama made a good point.

"Well, I guess the people riding it do look pretty secure." She saw kids *laughing* with their *hands in the air.*

"That's right," said Mama. "We can sit here and watch, but *you won't see anyone flying out*."

Miriam laughed. "I guess when I look at the facts and ask the right questions, I shouldn't be worried...

... But let's go see the animals first so we don't run out of time."

"Horsey! Horsey!" Miriam's little sister shouted as she ran toward the first pen.

"Sara, slow down! You'll startle the horse and start a stampede," scolded Miriam, always feeling responsible for her siblings.

Miriam turned around and saw a girl about her age walking toward them.

"Spot doesn't startle easily. *Some horses do though*, the jumpy ones that seem like they're always ready to run off and hide. Spot's mama was like that, but my Abuela calmed her down and turned her into the **BEST** therapy horse in all of Royce County. Abuela says she just needed to **LEARN TO SORT THE MAIL**, *you know*, to learn the difference between important messages and junk mail when her brain said, '**DANGER**.'"

Miriam stood with her mouth open. It isn't often she meets someone who talks this much!

"I'm sorry! I forgot my manners. **I'm Gabby**," said the girl.

"Hi. **I'm Miriam.** This is my sister, Sara...

"I think I'm just like that horse you're talking about. My brain is always *SHOUTING*,

'Danger! Danger!'

"But this one's okay? She won't bite or kick?" Her sister reached up as Spot turned her head. "... **Sara!** *DON'T...*" Miriam took a deep breath to stop and think.

Miriam **looked at the facts.** *The horse is in a pen.*
It is being shown by a child, so it must be good with
kids. Her mom and dad were also there to keep
Sara safe. That wasn't her responsibility right now.

She already **asked the right questions.**
Gabby told her the horse won't bite or kick.

"**LASSo your worry**, Miriam,
SORT THE MAIL," she told herself.
The danger messages her brain was sending
were junk mail right now.

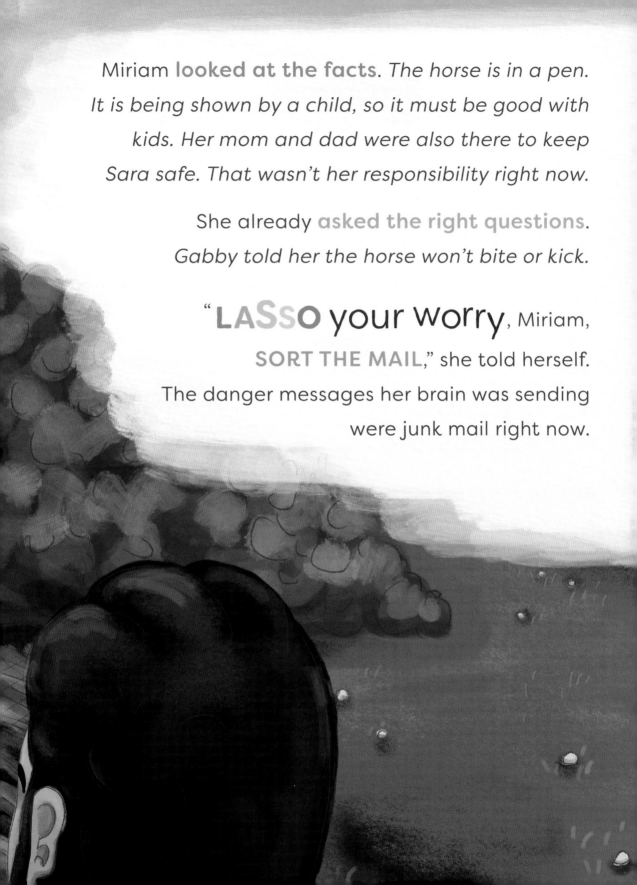

Miriam relaxed *just enough* to enjoy meeting her new friend.

"I have an idea," said Gabby. "Let's go see the *exotic animals*! My neighbor, Mr. Frank, has some really interesting pets! They're just around the corner."

"May I, Baba?"
Miriam asked.

"Sure. Mama will watch
from the corner, and we'll
stay right here. Come
back to us as soon as
you're finished,"
replied her dad.

"Mr. Frank!"
shouted Gabby when she caught sight of her neighbor. "This is my new friend, Miriam. She's from the city, and I wanted to show her your animals."

"Nice to meet you, Miriam," said Mr. Frank. "This is Calissa. Don't worry. She loves kids. You can pet her."

"Oh, I *love* camels! Where my family is from, camels are known for peace and confidence. They're calm even in the middle of a sandstorm..."

...As the words came out of her mouth, Miriam realized that if her worry were like a sandstorm, she just needed to find the peace and calm of a camel to get through it.

People can't do anything in a sandstorm because the sand just gets everywhere – in their eyes, their ears, even up their noses!

Worry can disable a person like that, too, make you want to curl up with your eyes shut and do nothing.

"Camels' eyes have three eyelids to keep the sand out," *Miriam continued.* "One is clear so they can close it all the way and still see!

Isn't that *amazing*?

They can even close their nostrils!"

Gabby pinched her nose and sucked in to keep her nostrils closed. The girls exploded with laughter! A good laugh helps release worries and Miriam felt more relaxed.

"Thank you, Calissa, for helping me find calm in the storm. I'm going to **LASSO** my worry and **SET LIMITS,** shut it out and move on with my day." Quietly she thought, "Thank you, Worry. You've done your job to help me think through dangers. I don't need you any more tonight. You just stay right here." And she swept the worries off of her shoulders and blew them into the pen with Calissa.

"She can handle it,"

Miriam giggled to herself.

Feeling
confident,
Miriam asked,
"Gabby, do you
want to go ride the
Whirly Cups?"

"Sure!"
exclaimed Gabby.
"I would
love to!"

As they came back around the corner, Miriam's parents were *right where they said they would be*, now joined by Gabby's mom.

"Mama, Baba, guess what! Worry won't keep me from having fun today! I've set limits and **LASSO**ed my worry whirlwind," Miriam exclaimed.

"Now I'm ready
to conquer the
Whirly Cups!"

"Can we go too, please?"
echoed Gabby.

"Absolutely!"
Gabby's mom replied.

Lights flashed and music started to play
as the Whirly Cups began to spin.
Miriam was feeling *worried* again.

"Oh no!"

She told Gabby.
"I wish I hadn't come."

"Here," said Gabby as she comforted her new friend. "Take my hand, and we'll make it through together!"

Miriam understood what her parents had been practicing with her all along.

"**LASSO your worry**," she told herself.

"OVERCOME WORRY WITH COMFORT."

With a friend by her side, she felt her worry whirlwind blow away.

Overcome worry with comfort

When your mind is in a tizzy,

you feel butterflies all frenzied

and the worry whirlwind's on the loose -

Quick! LASSO your worry

and trap it in a hurry

before the worry whirlwind lassoes you!

———

You can be like Miriam and learn to

Lasso your worry too. Lasso is an acronym.

That is a way to remember important things.

Each of the letters stands for something important.

To **LASSO** your worry you can:

 LOOK AT THE FACTS before you act

 ASK THE RIGHT QUESTIONS, too.

 SORT THE MAIL; toss out the junk

SET LIMITS when worry's job is done,

then you...

 OVERCOME WORRY WITH COMFORT!

LEARN & DISCUSS

*Take the content of the book further! **LEARN** to understand worry then **DISCUSS** with your child.*

 Anxiety often increases in the elementary years as children become more aware of the world around them and can think creatively about scenarios of disaster. Anxiety over new situations is common, as well as worries about both real and imagined dangers. Many elementary aged children are still struggling to understand what is real versus imaginary, so remote dangers and imaginary threats are common worries. Make sure the media your child sees and interacts with is not promoting additional anxiety.

As Miriam's family drove to the County Fair, she started to think about all of her worries. What kinds of things do you worry about when you have time alone to think? Do you worry often? Do you sometimes start out being excited about something only to realize you're actually really worried about it?

 Worry is often manifested in physical symptoms because it can activate the protective fight or flight response. It may produce some or all of the following symptoms: racing heart, cold or numb hands and feet, light-headedness, disorientation, feeling out of breath, nausea and headaches. Anxiety and anger are closely related because of the fight or flight response and some children appear angry when they are anxious. Get to know your child's signals so you can be ready to handle worry as soon as it comes up. Often a child will not be able to talk through worries while the perceived threat is near. Taking deep breaths, exercise, rocking and other soothing activities will bring your child's body back into a state that can process the event.

Miriam's head felt dizzy and her stomach was hurting because of all her worry. How does your body feel when you're worried?

 Help your child look at the facts behind their fears. Let your child be the detective, searching for facts and truths that bring safety. Once your child has identified the facts of a situation he can feel prepared, not scared about the experience. Develop a safety plan or an action plan for scenarios that regularly worry your child.

When Miriam was worried about getting lost at the county fair, her parents helped her remember the facts. They had never been separated before and they had a good safety plan. When and where do you feel the safest? What helps you feel safe in a new place? Would making a safety plan help with any of your worries?

LOOK AT THE FACTS

Turning worry into a question helps determine the level of actual threat in a situation. If a child says, "I'm going to fail the test," teach your child to ask, "Will I really fail?" or "Why do I think I will fail?" and prompt them to answer as if they are comforting someone else.

Miriam's family helped her ask questions about her fears and she saw that she didn't need to be worried. What questions can you ask next time you're worried?

It is faulty thinking, or "junk mail" that traps a child in a worry whirlwind. Do an exercise with your child to illustrate the difference between good mail and junk mail. Allow your child to check the mail with you and demonstrate what makes mail important or "junk mail." Just as your child will be able to sort your actual mail after doing it with you many times, with practice, your child can learn to detect the mistakes in their thinking on their own. (If you are parenting a child who has experienced trauma, be sure you're sensitive to their past. Some of their worst fears may have been realized before. Calling those signals "junk mail" may discredit their experience. Use the terms "needed" and "not needed" instead.)

Your feelings are always sending you messages that you need to sort, like mail, before reacting. Sometimes warning messages are important, but sometimes they are junk mail and we need to toss the thought in the trash. Tell me a time when a "danger" message is helpful. Tell me a time when a "danger" message would be junk mail.

Worry's job is to alert us about potential dangers, but does not need to take away from safe fun. Don't let worry out of its proper place. Asking "is this the place/time for that worry?" may help your child evaluate whether the concerns are appropriate to the situation. You may gain insight into how your child is best comforted by pretending to be worried and allowing your child to comfort you.

Everybody has a job, but jobs have limits. The delivery man brings our pizza, but is it appropriate for him to FEED you the pizza? No! Worry is like that, too. Its job is to help us find danger, but it isn't supposed to keep us from having safe fun. After worry does its job, if there isn't any real danger, you can tell worry, "No, thank you! Stay here and don't follow me!"

Some children are more easily comforted than others. If your child is often anxious, keep comfort items on hand, such as a special toy or security item, when going into an anxious situation. A promised reward following a courageous act can also be a comforting thought in the midst of worry. You may pretend to be worried and let your child comfort you. This will give you insight into how the child is best comforted.

Miriam's new friend went with her on the ride. It helped her feel brave.
When you feel worried, whom do you want to have with you?
What makes you feel better when you're worried?

*For additional tip and reference information visit **www.realMVPkids.com**.*

ASK THE RIGHT QUESTIONS

SORT THE MAIL

SET LIMITS

OVERCOME WORRY WITH COMFORT

Meet the

mvpkids®

featured in

Miriam Lassoes the Worry Whirlwind™

MIRIAM NASSER

GABBY GONZALEZ

Can you also find these MVP Kids®?

EZEKIEL JORDAN

FAITH JORDAN

YONG CHEN

Also featuring...

DR. ABDUL NASSER
"Baba"

MRS. SALMA NASSER
"Mama"

SARA NASSER
Sister

ADAM NASSER
Brother

MRS. MARIA GONZALEZ
Gabby's Mom

YONG CHEN

LEO RUSSO

FRANKIE RUSSO

JULIA ROJAS

GABBY GONZALEZ

ANNIE JAMES

AANYA PATEL

BLAKE JAMES

SARA COHEN-GOLDSTEIN